Maggie Durran's work with children began with several years as a school teacher. Since then she has organised children's programmes at a variety of camps, conferences and playschemes. She has written drama, stories and songs for children. She spends a lot of time talking to adults about children; her books include *Beginnings* and *Hello, I'm a person too*. She has one child of her own, Jacqueline.

dear god
Most of the
time your
quite nice

compiled by Maggie Durran

Fount Paperbacks
Collins

First published in Great Britain in 1985
by Fount Paperbacks, London

Photographs reproduced by kind
permission of the following:

Derek Coley 85, 113
John Hawkins 36
Sarah Hedley 43, 44, 69, 104, 108
Neils McGuinness 61
Patrick Mortemore 32, 59, 117
Salvation Army 95
Rosemary Sandberg 45, 80, 103
Janine Wiedel 72
All other photography by Sally Munt
Cover illustration: Max Baird-Smith

Made and printed in Great Britain by
William Collins Sons & Co. Ltd, Glasgow

Introduction

In their quiet moments our children have many reflections on life. The images and experiences are a kaleidoscope that is sifted and rationalised to fit their own way of thinking. In the same way their experience of God and the words they hear about God are fitted to their particular understanding of life. Idiosyncratic maybe, but we are amused as much with the reflection of ourselves in the children's words as with the children's spontaneous and original humour.

I am sure God is as attentive to each of these children's sayings, with their reverence and earnestness, as he is to the grandest rhetoric in the greatest cathedral. So I share with you the prayers and pictures of God that the children gave me so that we can all be a little enriched.

Maggie Durran

Contents

With thanks to the children

Christopher Mark Rupert Fiona Darren Judy Christo
Esther Alan Sally Margo Matthew Hannah David
Lydia Rebecca Jenny Jane Bethany Annabel Miriam
Nick Luke Graham Alexander Rebecca Sarah Alice
Archie Max Christopher Campbell

Our Father God

God is nearly up to the sky, bigger than the trees, he is around all of us.
Sally

I don't think he's got any feet, he's just to his waist.

David

He has lots of little
people sitting in his
hands all the people
in heaven

Lydia

I wonder who is God's
and Jesus's mummies.
Alan

I think God's favourite programme
would be tom and Jerry and
cartoons because he'll need some
fun up there.
Judy

His feet are the mountains and his head is the clouds. He dances to pop music and the whole earth rocks and shakes.

Rebecca

God takes the babies out
of the jars and puts them
in the mummies tummies.

Christo

I don't think Jesus is
God though I think
they are married to
each other. David

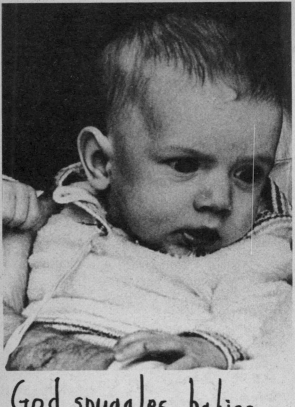

God snuggles babies
and rocks them in his
rocking chair and at
night puts them to sleep.
Sally

Who lives in heaven

Heaven is a good place to be if you're dead. It is a dead house. The dead people just lay down with their eyes shut.

Margo

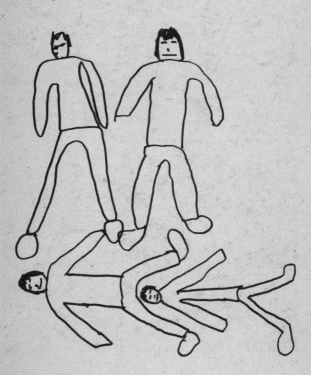

Heaven is on top of a cloud but you can't see it. You can go anywhere at all and you won't fall off. It goes on and on and on and on and on.

Christopher

Sometimes if you walk along you
think you are upside down cos you
are on the bottom of the earth so
you are scared you may be falling
off the ground. We are on the top. I
reckon heaven will be on the top as
well, so the sun will shine on it to
give it light.

David

In heaven there won't be any beds,
just a blank space all filled up with
people with candles in their hands.

Alan

Angels are Like people
with wings and no Feet.
One of them has a star
on her Dress   Bethany

Dear God
People tell us heaven is in the sky
but when you go up in an aeroplane
you look for it but it isn't there. It
must be invisible.

Darren

Christopher: I think heaven is higher than space. It's the highest thing in the world.
Alan: You can't get further than space!
Christopher: You can't get further than heaven! Space doesn't go on for ever it stops at heaven.

Heaven is much bigger than everything, than the whole universe. It has to be big to fit God and all the angels in. If God stood in front of us now I would probably only be able to see the bottom of his big toe.

Judy

Angels wear the same clothes
as us some people think they
are all Ladies, but they are men
as well.

christopher

People aren't buried in jeans and
things, they wear coffin robes
so that's what they wear in
heaven. Though i suppose they
might wear fig leaves. Fiona

People do gardening
in heaven and
have nice gardens
but they don't mow
the lawns. those
just grow and grow.

Fiona

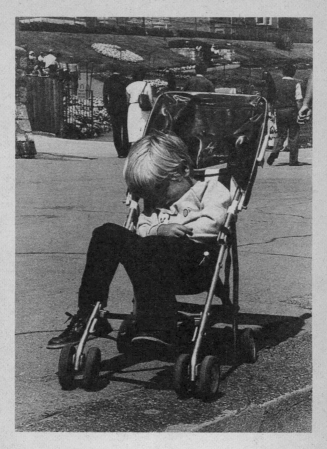

I can't imagine we'll be just lying there having a heavenly rest.

Esther

Dear God
In heaven I would like to play
football and the angels could be the
goalkeepers and just save it. They
could vanish then wherever you
kick they could move there.

Alan

Heaven must have swimming pools
and magical things like magic fruit
on trees and fruit you can't grow in
England or anywhere else in the
world.

Mark

In heaven you can eat anything except people. If there was a cannonball Christian he wouldn't be allowed to eat people. He might be allowed to eat evil ones as long as their souls still went down to hell.

Rebecca

God shows the angels how to eat Spaghetti

Alan

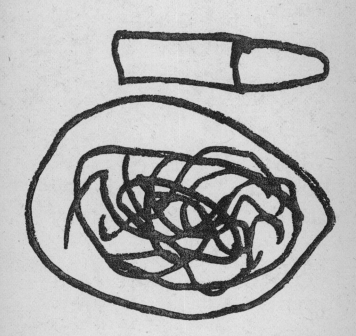

Heaven is like here
all over again
Lydia

We like you,
we worship you

Dear God
I'm glad you made giraffes and
hippopotamuses, they're nice, but
not mosquitos and fleas and spiders
and anteaters or snakes. I don't
mind lions when they are in cages.

Lydia

Dear God
I like all sorts of weather. When it's foggy you're inside the cloud, it's magical and it makes you feel you need glasses.

Mark

Dear God
Why did you make worms I
wonder? They're Godly birdfood.

Esther

Dear God
I specially like the world you made.
I like getting out and running in the
country side but I don't like it when
I am in the car I feel sick.

David

Dear God
If you came back now
you would have to have a
new name because we couldn't
call you uncle Jesus, could
we?
Jenny

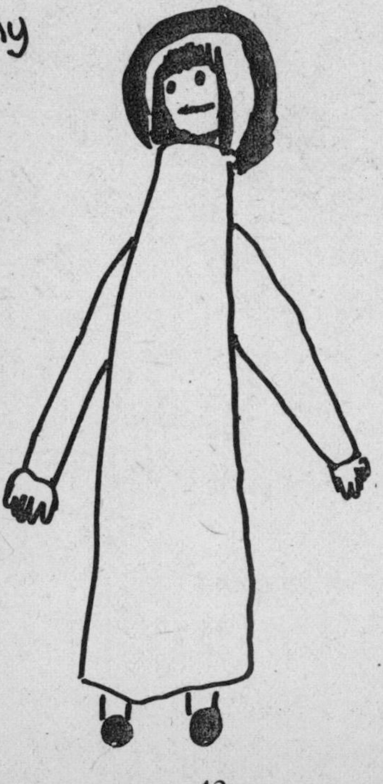

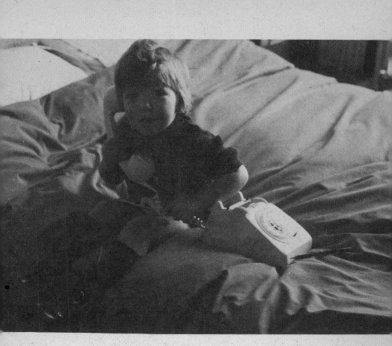

Dear God
some of the time your really
horrible But most of the
time your quite nice.

love From mark

He likes disco dancing. They have gigantic dances and the angels play harps for the music. Sometimes it's rock music but usually they play old slow songs to dance to.

Judy

Dear God
If every sort of flower was green and you got a bunch for your mummy it would be dull. I like colours best if they're nice and bright.
Mark

In the olden days people used to sacrifice animals to God. But if you had a farm and you kept on sacrificing you soon wouldn't have any animals left.

Mark

Your Kingdom come

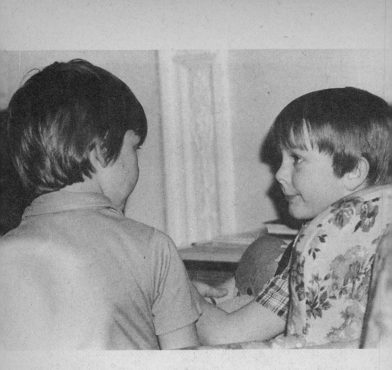

Darren: I reckon kings and queens
and ministers and special people
will see Jesus first.
Christopher: No! I reckon the poor
people will see Jesus first.
Darren: But if the queen was at the
back all the crowd would part and
let her through to the front anyway.

Dear God
Please make Jesus come
again while I am alive and
not too old. If I was old I
could hardly get through
the crowd.
Darren.

49

Dear God
I am glad Jesus came at
christmas or it would be
boring.

christo

Dear God
Once there was a feast and all the
rich people went near to Jesus and
all the poor people went on a far
table, away from Jesus by the cold
damp windows. Jesus told them to
swop over tables. I'd wish I was a
poor man then to get swopped onto
the best table, but people would
make fun of me afterwards.

Darren

Dear God
I don't think anyone should get
more money than anyone else
unless they do more work. Children
work very hard, harder than the
teachers but they don't get paid at
all. We should get at least five
pounds.

Darren

Your will be done

Dear God
If we just keep your laws and not
the other laws, like the law that we
have to walk on the pavement and
not on the road, and we walked on
the road we'd be chucked in prison!

Darren

He doesn't like love songs because mummy and daddy don't. He doesn't like tight jeans and miniskirts either or bikinis. He prefers old styles. But he does like soppy films like the Pink Panther.

Rebecca

Dear God I'm not sure if you like the queen ruling, arent the ten commandments the only kind of rules. —

Alan

Dear God   I will
tell all the people to
be good for you

christopher

Dear God
I will try not to tell
too many lies
David

Give us today

God opened the Kingdom door and stuck out his hand and put sweets in my mouth.

Sally

Dear God help
me to learn
from other
people. Sarah

Dear God
Please make me so I can stop the wind and the waves. I'd say stop and they'd stop. Jesus could do that and I want to know if there's people inside the waves that made them stop.

Darren

Daer GoD I
Wowld like 3 wishes
Love Luke.

Dear God

I'd like you to make
trees with flowers on
the top.

Christopher

I ask God things inside my head and he can mindread and it worked once. I asked him for some dominoes and I got some Pooh Bear ones.

Mark

DEAR JESUS, I WOULD
LIKE EVERYTHING
I LIKE. LOVE, GrAHAM

Dear God
I'd like you to fix
a robot to do my
washing up.
Darren

Dear God
I'd like you to give me
the brains to invent engines
for the carts I've already
invented. That would be best.
Mark

PS you could invent something
For me and drop it down or
Put it in t shops quite cheaply
So Mummy and Daddy could
buy it

Dear God
I'd like you to get me
into a real adventure.
Alan

Dear God
I'd like you to get rid of money, it causes too many problems like I run out of it too quickly.

Lydia

Dear God
i'd like to see you
in heaven.
love
christopher.

Dear God
I would like you to make the queen
visit me then I could ask her if she
had any gold and if she said yes, I'd
say Can I have some please?

Darren

Dear God
please don't change
school. I'm bored
when there isn't
any.
　　　Lydia

Dear God
I wish you would make us
so we could see directly
into each others minds. It
would save the t.v.
Esther

For our friends

Dear God
My cats would like you
to make them bigger so
they can chase dogs round
love From christo.

Dear God I'd like everyone to have the Same amount of money so there's no robbers love Hannah

Dear God
Please make all the owls
tame and friendly.

Miriam

Please forgive us

Dear God

If I were you and I
made a world like
this and people messed
it up I would be sad
                    Jane

We make God angry.

Esther

Dear God
I think you must be cross about
zoos because the animals are all
locked up. I don't think lions would
hurt you if they weren't locked up
all the time.

Christopher

Dear God
I'm thakfull for everything
you did and if I don't act
like I am or do anything wrong
please forgive me.

Rebecca.

dear god if you
were here now
you might tell
me off. Lydia

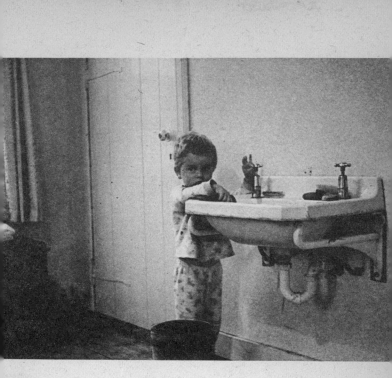

Dear God
I think you love us when we are
naughty. I wouldn't love anyone
when they are naughty. Our mum
loves us when we are naughty. And
our dad. I reckon our grans and
aunties and uncles love us when we
are naughty as well.

Darren

Dear God
I hope everyone in heaven
is perfect. if you
are trying to climb a tree
they wouldn't push you
down like sometimes
people do.
Mark

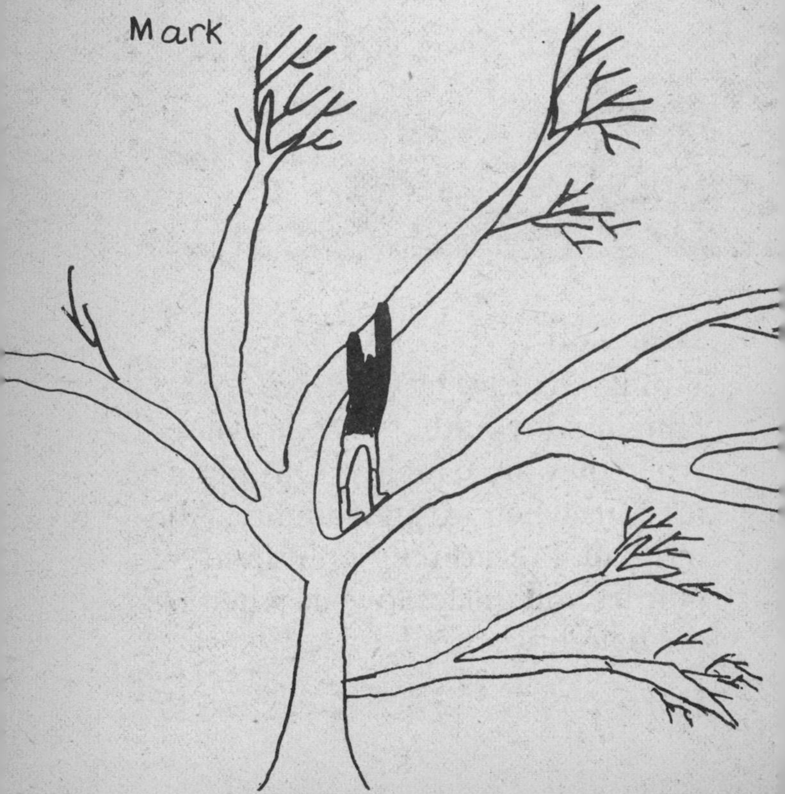

Dear God
The world isn't how it was when
you drowned it, there's more
foolish people now. It's worse now.

Fiona

In the bible people made all their metal into a gold idol, and God nearly killed the whole lot of them. So I don't think his temper could hold over people blowing up the whole world with bombs.

Esther

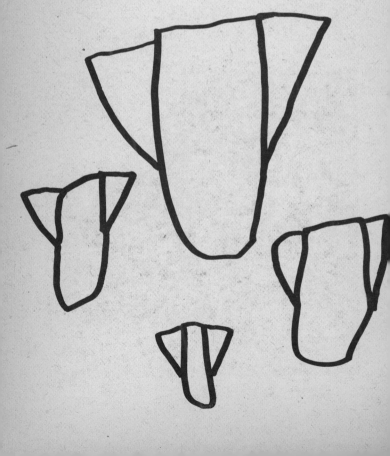

Lead us not
into temptation

Dear God
The devil thinks he is
the right way and Jesus
is the wrong way   Alan

Dear God

I suppose I could ask you
to make me perfect But
I wouldn't have any
friends cos I'd never get
into trouble like they wo
would. Better really not
be perfect.

Mark

In heaven if you do steal something
God doesn't kill you he opens a flap
and you just fall through the ground
to hell.

Darren

In heaven they are all perfect, but mind you they tell lies sometimes, everyone tells lies sometimes.

David

In heaven there will be some money so if you want to see Jesus on a special occasion, to tell him something that is secret you could pay some money to go in to see him at the middle of the month.

Darren

But deliver us
from evil

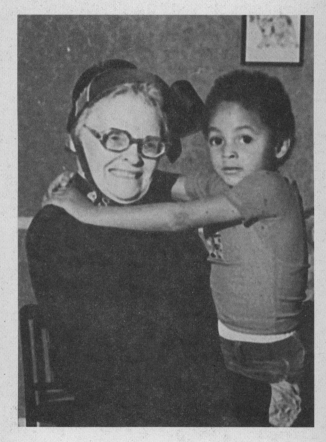

Hell is all nasty and they hit you if you don't do the work and it's all red and black and purple and they've all got nits.

Christopher

Hell would be nasty for children but I think God makes everyone grownup before heaven or hell so there's no children in heaven or hell.

Christo

Dear God

I don't think Jesus will Kill
The devil cos I think Jesus
is perfect and if he Killed
the devil he won't be
perfect anymore.
Christopher

If you are very good in hell God will help you to escape he'll give you a secret message.

Alan

In hell there'll be massive fire there with all people dancing round it and black smoke everywhere. And there's a black chair with the devil sitting on it watching the people dance and telling them what to do.

Darren

Glorious powerful
King forever

At Christmas God gets tired of fighting the devil so he stops.

Margo

Dear God

Can you tell me what forever is
because no-one else can?
Mary

Jesus looks over one half of the
world and God looks over the
other.

Christopher

Dear God
It makes me cross that there are all
these droughts and you don't seem
to be doing anything about them.
Then there's floods in other places,
like all this rain we are getting so
why can't you send it half way
round the world. It seems
ridiculous.

David

God made the sky and it's so long it even goes to London.

Margo

Dear God
I would like to see if
you have a special
sledge with angels at
the front pulling so
you can ride around
all gold with
dimonds on it.
Darren

All these things I grumble to you about I think there's probably a good reason for them. After all you are perfect so I shouldn't worry about it much as you'll get it straight somewhere or other.

Esther .

Dear God
I wonder if you still wear
rags or fine golden clothes

Christopher

Dear God
I'd like to live in your house
very much because it would
be tidy all the time.

Christopher

Dear God
I'd like to find something to tell you
that you don't know but you know
everything, cos you've looked down
on everything since the world
began.

Mark

Dear God
I want to know who made
you and what the world was
like when you were made.
            Darren.

Dear God
My teacher says its inpossible
that Adam and Eve happened
I think its more impossible that
all the universe is here with
no God to make it Esther

Dear God
I wonder why you made
animals that eat people.
From Christo

Motor cars and rich people
are mean to small children
and don't even share
things with us, that's why
all of them go to hell.
                    Christo

God speaks to us but we just don't hear him. We would have to go somewhere very still and quiet and concentrate on him. I haven't done it but I hope he will speak to me.

Alan

Dear God
Why did you make owls
sleep in the day and Hoot
and keep us awake.
Nicholas

Darren: I want to know how Jesus got up there, did he just disappear and go up.

Christopher: I think he just rised up a bit like Superman when his robes caught in the wind.

Darren: He may have had on purple robes and all the air went up with him.

Christopher: I don't think God pulled him up on a string though. It would have been a very long piece of string anyway.

Dear God
You shouldn't have made very
greedy people. Like in Robin Hood
there's a lot of poor people and the
Sheriff of Nottingham made them
pay extra taxes so they got poorer
and poorer. Greedy is alright but
not very very greedy people.

Mark

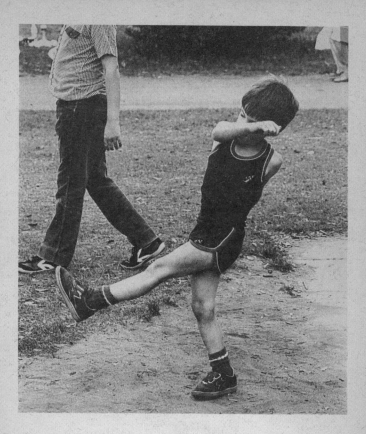

Dear God
When I am gloomy or
down it the dumps you
could start speaking
to me and make me happy
Mark

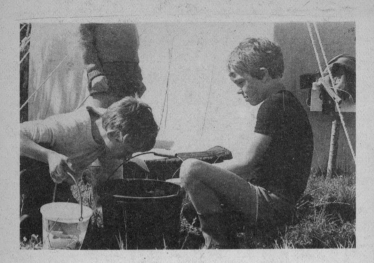

Dear God
Toads are very funny
creatures to have made.
Rupert

Dear God
Your favourite colour must be
green because you made nearly
everything green, didn't you?

Fiona

He likes comedy things like batman and superman.

Darren

God must be quite rich to have all
those angels for servants.

Darren

Dear God
if you walked in now and said
"Hello I'm God" I'd say
"Stop pulling my leg!"
    Judy.